Orthodoxy for Children

Fr. Anthony Borisov

Fasting

**Illustrations by
Victoria Kitavina**

Grand Rapids · Exaltation Press · 2020

Copyright © 2020 Exaltation Press

Author: Fr. Anthony Borisov
Illustrator: Victoria Kitavina
Translator: Fr. John Hogg

"Fasting"
 This book is designed to help children understand the purpose of fasting in the Orthodox Church. It begins by talking about the difference between dieting for health reasons and fasting for God. It then looks at the Church calendar, noting when and why we fast, and explaining what is more important than food in order to fast in a God-pleasing way.

All rights reserved. This book or any portion thereof may not be reproduced or used in any manner whatsoever without the express written permission of the publisher except for the use of brief quotations in a book review.

Translated from the original "О Постах" by Nikea Press, Copyright © Trading house «NIKEA», www.Nikeabooks.ru

ISBN: 978-1-950067-15-2 (Paperback)

Edited by Cynthia Hogg
Graphical editing by Emily Harju

First printing edition 2020

Exaltation Press
Grand Rapids, MI

www.ExaltationPress.com

For bulk orders, please contact editor@exaltationpress.com.

Table of Contents

FOOD AND DIET 4
WHEN CHRIST FASTED 6
CHRIST IN THE DESERT 8
FASTING AS IMITATION OF THE WORK OF CHRIST 10
THE CHURCH'S FOUR FASTING SEASONS 12
WEDNESDAY AND FRIDAY FASTING 14
FASTING ON FEAST DAYS 16
PREPARATION FOR COMMUNION 18
FASTING IS A TIME TO DO GOOD 22
FASTING AS SELF-EXAMINATION 24
WHICH FOOD IS FASTING AND WHICH IS NOT? 26
THE PRAYER OF ST. EPHREM THE SYRIAN 28
FASTING AND FORGIVENESS 30
FASTING IS A PATH LEADING TO FREEDOM 32

FOOD AND DIET

Many centuries ago, there was a famous doctor named Hippocrates who lived in Greece. People respected him for his ability to treat different diseases. He was also respected for the great wisdom he possessed. He not only treated people who were sick, but each time, he wrote down what they were suffering from and how he had helped them recover. Thanks to Hippocrates, the first books of medicine appeared and actually, the science of medicine itself! Can you believe that even modern doctors respect this ancient doctor so much that when they become doctors, they solemnly make a vow that was written by him? It is called the "Hippocratic Oath." Hippocrates left us many useful pieces of advice. One of them is that we should pay close attention to what we eat. Instead of medicine, Hippocrates often told his patients to eat a proper diet.

From the Hippocratic Oath:

"I will prescribe treatment for the sick according to my strength and abilities, never doing them any harm or injury."

Hippocrates

"Let food be your medicine."

Hippocrates

"Fasting is the mother of bodily health, as well."

St. John Chrysostom

5 Fasting

Hippocrates lived at a time when many others had stopped taking care of their health. They ate a lot of food (often, very bad food) and didn't get much exercise. The result was just as bad as you might expect. People were in pain and suffering from different kinds of diseases, but they didn't listen to Hippocrates. It was hard for them to give up their favorite foods. It might not seem hard. After all, how hard is it to not eat pie or candy? In reality, however, giving up a favorite food takes real effort and is a real test of our will. Among the ancient Greeks, however, there were some who listened to Hippocrates and ate only healthy food. Soon, they noticed that their health was improving and the illnesses were leaving them. For the first time, there was a diet to bring health.

WHEN CHRIST FASTED

Centuries passed and in a country called Judea, the Savior of the world was born, Jesus Christ. He wasn't just an ordinary man, but God, who had taken on our nature. The Son of God became one of the residents of Judea. The Savior could work great miracles (for example, He could walk on water), but His body was very real. It needed food and drink and rest. Until He was thirty years old, Christ lived in the city of Nazareth. Then, He began to travel all over Judea, preaching His new teaching. We call His teaching the Gospel, which means "good news." Before He began His mission, Christ went out into the desert for forty days. Can you imagine it? While He was there, He didn't eat anything. The Savior didn't give up food because He was ill and needed to stick to a healthy diet (like Hippocrates would suggest). No. When Christ turned away from food, He did so because He had decided to undertake a great spiritual labor. He decided to fast.

> "Christ fasted not because He needed to fast, but in order to teach us."
>
> "Just like a bird cannot fly without the help of wings, so fasting cannot succeed without its two wings: prayer and giving alms."
>
> *St. John Chrysostom*

7 Fasting

CHRIST IN THE DESERT

Christ's time in the desert was a difficult test for Him. When His bodily strength began to leave Him, an evil spirit appeared - the Devil. The Devil decided to make use of the fact that Christ had grown weak after being hungry for so long. The Devil began to tempt Christ, suggesting different sinful actions for Him to do. However, something unexpected happened. The evil spirit hadn't taken something into account. Yes, the Savior's body was exhausted from fasting but His spirit had only grown stronger. It says in the Bible that Christ spent the whole forty days praying constantly to His Father. Going without food only made His prayer stronger. When the Devil appeared, he had no chance of defeating Christ. The forty-day fast had spiritually strengthened the Savior. He firmly rejected all of the Devil's temptations. The evil spirit was left with nothing.

> "This kind (the Devil and his servants) can only be cast out by prayer and fasting."
>
> *Matthew 17:21*
>
> "Whoever has hatred and condemnation in their heart, let them first cleanse their soul and then come and fast and pray."
>
> *St. Ephrem the Syrian*

9 Fasting

FASTING AS IMITATION OF THE WORK OF CHRIST

Jesus Christ had many disciples. All of them tried to imitate their Teacher, including through the labor of fasting. Because of that, long ago, when the Christian Church had only just appeared, a tradition was born: the tradition of limiting the food we eat for forty days, like Christ did when He was in the desert. Early Christians kept a forty-day fast once a year, fasting all together. That was how they prepared themselves for the Church's biggest feast - Holy Pascha, the glorious Resurrection of Christ. Some Christians went forty days without eating anything and only drank water. Others ate, but only a little. However, that wasn't what was most important. What was most important was that Christians spent the whole fast praying fervently to God and showing mercy to the people around them. They didn't see fasting as a kind of healthy diet. Rather, it is a means that God gives us to help us become better and more pure.

One elder used to say to young monks: "When a general wants to take a city from his enemies, what does he do first? First, he cuts off the city's water and then its food. The enemy, being hungry, submits to the general. The same is true with our sins. If we live in prayer and fasting, all our sinful failings will grow weak and disappear."

"Christ our Lord rejoices in our fasting, only if we fast with love, hope, and faith."

St. Ephrem the Syrian

11 Fasting

THE CHURCH'S FOUR FASTING SEASONS

As time passed, four long fasts developed in the Orthodox Church. You already read about the most important one. The forty-day fast before Pascha is called Great Lent. It is the strictest and longest fast of the four. Almost as long and as important is the Nativity Fast. As you've probably guessed, this fast is to help get us ready for the Nativity of Christ, Christmas. Another one of the fasts is called the Dormition Fast. It lasts just two weeks and ends on the feast of the Dormition of the Theotokos on August 15th. The fourth fast is the Apostles' Fast, in honor of the holy Apostles Peter and Paul. The Apostles' Fast can last up to five weeks long. Its length depends on the day of Pascha that year. It ends on June 30th, the feast of the holy Apostles Peter and Paul.

"The fasts are given to us to keep us from being pampered and to prepare us to show mercy."

"You fast? Then ask forgiveness from those you have wronged, never envy your brother, and hate no one."

St. John Chrysostom

Yearly Cycle of Feasts and Fasts

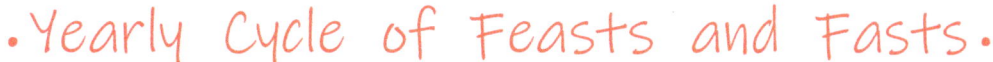

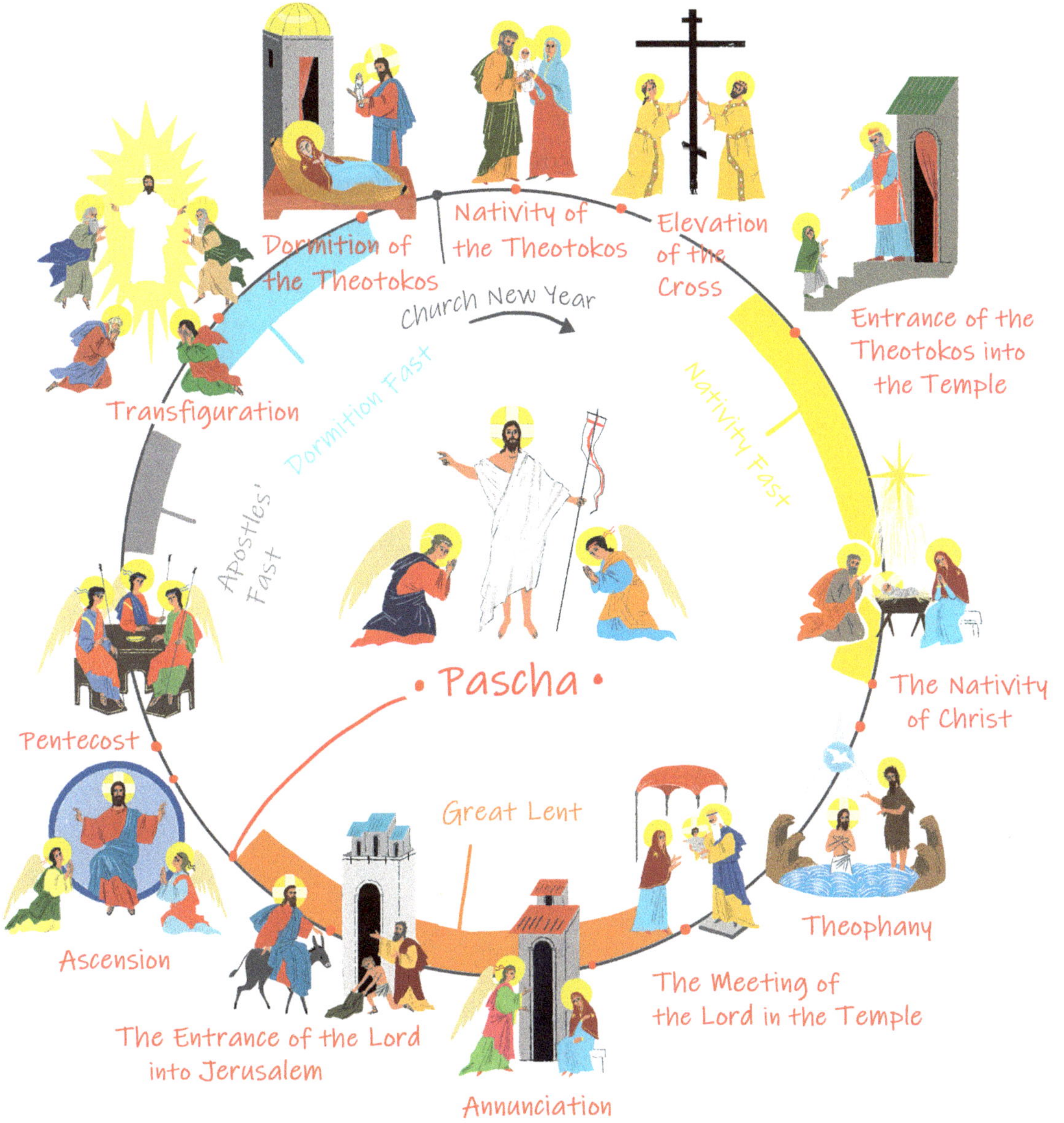

WEDNESDAY AND FRIDAY FASTING

> Once, a man set the goal of fasting for forty days, to make God appear to him. He stopped eating and locked himself in his house. Eventually, they found him weak and lying on the floor. "Well?" they asked. "Did you see God?" "No, I didn't see God but I did see my own foolishness."

Our Church has some regular fasts that are only a day long. These fasts also began many years ago. Orthodox Christians try to fast on Wednesday and Friday. These days are connected to the memory of the last week in the life of Jesus Christ. On Wednesday, Judas, His disciple, betrayed Him. For thirty pieces of silver, he agreed to lead the soldiers to Christ so they could seize Him. On Friday, Jesus Christ was executed when the Roman soldiers nailed Him to the Cross because they believed the false testimony of His enemies. Christ knew beforehand that He would be seized and crucified, but He didn't try to change His fate. He understood that His death would save all mankind and open the Kingdom of Heaven to us. When we fast on Wednesday and Friday, we show our veneration for the Savior's great work.

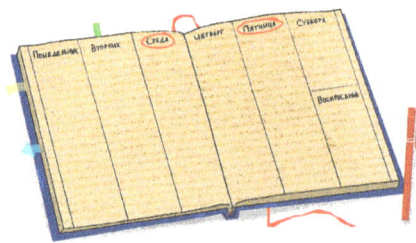

Fasting

"Whoever fasts sincerely and without hypocrisy imitates Christ and although he is still on earth, he is like the angels"

St. John Chrysostom

FASTING ON FEAST DAYS

Wednesday and Friday aren't the only one-day fasts. There are other days on the Church calendar when we fast no matter what day of the week they fall on. For example, there is the Eve of Theophany **(Jan 5th)**, the day before we celebrate the Baptism of Christ. That is how we end the Twelve Days of Christmas, the joyful time after Nativity. On the eve of Theophany, we fast to better prepare ourselves for the feast of Christ's Baptism.

There are also some fasts that fall on the day of a great feast; for example, the Exaltation of the Cross, which we celebrate on September 14th. A long time ago, on that day, the holy Empress Helen found the Cross of Jesus Christ in Jerusalem. Another fast that falls on a feast day is the Beheading of John the Baptist, on August 29th. This feast reminds us of how evil people killed a great saint, the prophet John the Baptist.

> "How wonderful is the work of fasting because it lightens our souls from the heaviness of sin!"
>
> *St. John Chrysostom*

17 Fasting

PREPARATION FOR COMMUNION

You probably have noticed another time when we fast. We fast when we are getting ourselves ready for Holy Communion by not eating or drinking anything in the morning before going to Church.

I remember reading about preparation for Communion for the first time in a book by Ivan Shmelyov, called *The Year of the Lord*. The main character decides to prepare himself for Communion during Great Lent. Notice, I didn't just say fast, but actually to prepare himself for Communion. To do that, he didn't just limit his food, but started to go to Church more often, too. He also gave away his allowance to the poor. So you see, preparation for Communion involves several things at once - fasting, prayer, and works of mercy. That is what the Lord expects from us. He doesn't just want us not to eat certain foods. The most important thing is that we dedicate our time to prayer and works of mercy.

> "Fasting should always be joined with prayer."
>
> *St. John Chrysostom*

Fasting

Orthodoxy for Children   20

21 Fasting

FASTING IS A TIME TO DO GOOD

> Imagine that a farmer has a small packet of wheat seeds. He plants them, gathers the harvest, and has more seeds than before. Now, instead of a small packet, he has a large one. Once again, he plants the wheat, gathers the harvest, and now has enough seeds to fill a whole sack. If he plants all these seeds, soon he will have enough to fill a whole barn. But if he doesn't plant the seeds, they will spoil. In order for the seeds to grow, he has to plant them. The farmer has to give them up to keep them. The same thing is true with love. For our love to grow, we have to give it to others.

In the last century, there was an Orthodox bishop living in England. His name was Metropolitan Anthony Bloom. Before he became a monk, he was a doctor. Already then, he had strong faith in God. Once, he was treating a little girl. Her parents didn't have enough money for a good hospital and so they were overjoyed when Anthony agreed to help them and began to treat her at home. He came regularly to check and see how the little girl was doing.

Finally, the little girl got better. Her parents were happy and they invited Anthony to come over to examine her one last time. They didn't know that he was fasting and so they prepared a very tasty dinner, a roast chicken. The future metropolitan knew that if he refused the food they were offering him, he would be rejecting the love of the girl's parents. He ate everything they put on his plate. Although he broke the fast, he did what was most important. He showed mercy and love to others.

23 Fasting

FASTING AS SELF-EXAMINATION

A friend of mine loves to go hiking. Over and over again, he sets off with a tent. In a week, he can travel fifty or even a hundred miles. He claims that it is how he tests himself to see if he has strength and endurance. There are other ways to test yourself, though.

> Once, a young monk came to see an elder, looking for advice, and said, "We have two monks in our monastery. One of them never leaves his cell. He prays constantly and fasts. The other goes to the hospital to help people. Which of their two lives is more pleasing to God?" The elder answered, "Even if the first were to fly, he still wouldn't exceed the virtue of the second, who cares for the sick."

For example, fasting is also a way of testing yourself. You don't believe me? Look closely. It's very easy to be kind and polite when everything is going well for you. Now imagine that for a while, you have to go without your favorite food and your favorite entertainment, too! What's the big deal, you wonder? Well, I think you might be able to make it a day or two. Then the real testing begins. Part of you will want to go back to the way things were but your conscience will tell you to be patient and wait a little longer. You'll need that patience or else you'll become so prickly that everyone around you will suffer for it. That is the real test, to fast and yet not to get angry.

25 Fasting

WHICH FOOD IS FASTING AND WHICH IS NOT?

When a fast begins, we give up certain kinds of foods. Most of all, we give up meat and dairy products. If the fast is very strict (like during Great Lent), we give up fish as well. The reason for this isn't because these food are bad for our health. Not at all. We fast as a spiritual labor that shows that we love, really love, and have faith in God.

I know people who give up their favorite foods (like pies and chocolates) during fasting times, even if the foods are fast friendly. I think that is a very good approach. When does an action really become a spiritual labor? When we have to overcome ourselves. Do you remember? Fasting isn't a diet for our health. It's a way of testing ourselves. Do we really love God? What is more important to us? To imitate Christ or to follow our ordinary way of life?

> A woman came to an old priest and said, "I want to move away from my relatives and live alone so that no one and nothing will stop me from fasting and praying."
>
> The old priest listened to her and said, "Did you know that the evil spirits don't eat and never sleep and yet they never get any better? Show mercy to your relatives and then God will receive both your fasting and your prayer."

> "What use is it for us to refrain from food if we do not chase out of our soul our bad habits?"
>
> *St. John Chrysostom*

27 Fasting

THE PRAYER OF ST. EPHREM THE SYRIAN

A long time ago, in the 4th century, there lived a great saint, Ephrem the Syrian. He was called "the Syrian" because he was ethnically Syrian. While he was still very young, St. Ephrem became a monk. He never married and he dedicated his life to the service of God. He was a very talented man who left behind many writings. His most well-known writing is a prayer that is said during Great Lent, called "the Prayer of St. Ephrem the Syrian," which is made up of three parts.

In the first part, we ask God to help us overcome laziness and despair. In the

---

The Prayer of St. Ephrem the Syrian

O Lord and Master of my life! Take from me the Spirit of sloth, despair, lust of power, and idle talk!
(Prostration)

But give rather a spirit of chastity, humility, patience, and love to Thy servant.
(Prostration)

Yea, O Lord and King! Grant me to see my own transgressions and not to judge my brother, for blessed art Thou unto ages of ages. Amen.
(Prostration)

O Master of my days! Do not give my soul a spirit of downcast idleness, of love of power (that hidden snake!) or of idle talk. Let me rather, O God, see my transgressions, that my brother may never receive condemnation from me! And enliven the spirit of humility, patience, love, and chastity within my heart!

Pushkin

second, we ask Him to give us instead the virtues, especially love. As the prayer ends, we ask God to allow us to see our own faults and, most importantly, not to judge others. The whole prayer reminds us that fasting is not the goal, but a means to an end, to help us grow in Christ.

FASTING AND FORGIVENESS

In order to begin fasting, there is one important condition that we have to meet first. Otherwise, our fasting will be meaningless, and turn into just another diet. The condition is this - you have to forgive those who have wronged you. And if you have wronged someone, you must ask them to forgive you. Why is this necessary?

Well, how can we begin a spiritual work if our hearts are weighed down with the rock of resentment? We fast so we can draw closer to God. Resentment doesn't let us do that but instead always drags us down. So if we don't begin with forgiveness, no matter what we give up when fasting, none of it will be helpful to us.

The day before the start of Great Lent, on Forgiveness Sunday, we have a special service at Church. It is called the Rite of Forgiveness, where we all ask each other's forgiveness so that we can enter the holy days of Lent with clean hearts.

> There once was a dove that kept moving from one nest to another. Each time, he found that he couldn't stand the strong, unpleasant smell coming from the new nest and so he kept moving on. Finally, he went to an old, experienced dove to complain about the smell. The old dove listened and then said, "Pay attention. Do you see how while you keep going from one nest to another, nothing ever changes? The unpleasant smell isn't coming from the nests but from you. If you want to make the world a better place, begin with yourself!"

31 Fasting

FASTING IS A PATH LEADING TO FREEDOM

Fasting isn't only a way for us to test ourselves. It is also a good opportunity for us to get rid of our bad habits. When I was a child, I knew a boy who loved playing computer games. He wasted a lot of time on them. As a result, he began to do poorly in school. It got so bad that after a while, his friends stopped hanging out with him. When they came over, he just sat and played his games.

Once, the boy realized that his life wasn't going in the right direction. As it happened, it was the beginning of Great Lent and so he decided that during Great Lent, he wouldn't play with his game console. He made it a few days before it started to be very difficult for him. Then, he remembered that fasting isn't just about giving up food but is also a time for prayer. He began to ask God to help him. The Lord heard him and gave him strength. He was able to keep the fast successfully. When Pascha came, he discovered that he didn't even want to play computer games anymore. Thanks to the fast, he was completely free of his bad habit! I want the same thing for you, my friend!

> "Fasting is a chariot leading us up to Heaven"
>
> *St. Ephrem the Syrian*